Police and Criminal Evidence Act 1984 (PACE)

CODE A
Revised

**CODE OF PRACTICE FOR THE EXERCISE BY:
POLICE OFFICERS OF STATUTORY POWERS
OF STOP AND SEARCH POLICE OFFICERS
AND POLICE STAFF OF REQUIREMENTS TO
RECORD PUBLIC ENCOUNTERS**

March 2015.

Commencement – Transitional Arrangements

This code applies to any search by a police officer and the recording of public encounters taking place after 00.00 on 19 March 2015.

GRAN*GIS* UK Publishing

Adapted and Published by GRANGIS (Grand Register Library).
Online: www.grangis.com.
E-mail: contact@grangis.com.

Contents

1.0 General

1.01 This code of practice must be readily available at all police stations for consultation by police officers, police staff, detained persons and members of the public.

1.02 The notes for guidance included are not provisions of this code, but are guidance to police officers and others about its application and interpretation. Provisions in the annexes to the code are provisions of this code.

1.03 This code governs the exercise by police officers of statutory powers to search a person or a vehicle without first making an arrest. The main stop and search powers to which this code applies are set out in Annex A, but that list should not be regarded as definitive (see Note 1). In addition, it covers requirements on police officers and police staff to record encounters not governed by statutory powers (see *paragraphs 2.11 and 4.12*). This code does not apply to:

(a) the powers of stop and search under:

(i) the Aviation Security Act 1982, section 27(2), and

(ii) the Police and Criminal Evidence Act 1984 (PACE), section 6(1) (which relates specifically to powers of constables employed by statutory undertakers on the premises of the statutory undertakers);

(b) searches carried out for the purposes of examination under Schedule 7 to the Terrorism Act 2000 and to which the Code of Practice issued under paragraph 6 of Schedule 14 to the Terrorism Act 2000 applies.

(c) the powers to search persons and vehicles and to stop and search in specified locations to which the Code of Practice issued under section 47AB of the Terrorism Act 2000 applies.

1 Principles governing stop and search

1.1 Powers to stop and search must be used fairly, responsibly, with respect for people being searched and without unlawful discrimination. Under the Equality Act 2010, section 149, when police officers are carrying out their functions, they also have a duty to have due regard to the need to eliminate unlawful discrimination, harassment and victimisation, to advance equality of opportunity between people who share a 'relevant protected characteristic' and people who do not share it, and to take steps to foster good relations between those persons (see *Notes 1 and 1A*). The Children Act 2004, section 11, also requires chief police officers and other specified persons and bodies to ensure that in the discharge of their functions they have regard to the need to safeguard and promote the welfare of all persons under the age of 18.

1.2 The intrusion on the liberty of the person stopped or searched must be brief and detention for the purposes of a search must take place at or near the location of the stop.

1.3 If these fundamental principles are not observed the use of powers to stop and search may be drawn into question. Failure to use the powers in the proper manner reduces their effectiveness. Stop and search can play an important role in the detection and prevention of crime, and using the powers fairly makes them more effective.

1.4 The primary purpose of stop and search powers is to enable officers to allay or confirm suspicions about individuals without exercising their power of arrest. Officers may be required to justify the use or authorisation of such powers, in relation both to individual searches and the overall pattern of their activity in this regard, to their supervisory officers or in court. Any misuse of the powers is likely to be harmful to policing and lead to mistrust of the police. Officers must also be able to explain their actions to the member of the public searched. The misuse of these powers can lead to disciplinary action (see *paragraphs 5.5 and 5.6*).

1.5 An officer must not search a person, even with his or her consent, where no power to search is applicable. Even where a person is prepared to submit to a search voluntarily, the person must not be searched unless the necessary legal power exists, and the search must be in accordance with the relevant power and the provisions of this Code. The only exception, where an officer does not require a specific power, applies to searches of persons entering sports grounds or other premises carried out with their consent given as a condition of entry.

1.6 Evidence obtained from a search to which this Code applies may be open to challenge if the provisions of this Code are not observed.

2 Types of stop and search powers

2.1 This code applies, subject to paragraph 1.03, to powers of stop and search as follows:

(a) powers which require reasonable grounds for suspicion, before they may be exercised; that articles unlawfully obtained or possessed are being carried such as section 1 of PACE for stolen and prohibited articles and section 23 of the Misuse of Drugs Act 1971 for controlled drugs;

(b) authorised under section 60 of the Criminal Justice and Public Order Act 1994, based upon a reasonable belief that incidents involving serious violence may take place or that people are carrying dangerous instruments or offensive weapons within any locality in the police area, or that it is expedient to use the powers to find such instruments or weapons that have been used in incidents of serious violence;

(c) *Not used;*

(d) the powers in Schedule 5 to the Terrorism Prevention and Investigation Measures (TPIM) Act 2011 to search an individual who has not been arrested, conferred by:

   (i) paragraph 6(2)(a) at the time of serving a TPIM notice;

   (ii) paragraph 8(2)(a) under a search warrant for compliance purposes; and

   (iii) paragraph 10 for public safety purposes.

   See *paragraph 2.18A.*

(e) powers to search a person who has not been arrested in the exercise of a power to search premises (see Code B *paragraph 2.4*).

(a) Stop and search powers requiring reasonable grounds for suspicion – explanation

General

2.2   Reasonable grounds for suspicion is the legal test which a police officer must satisfy before they can stop and detain individuals or vehicles to search them under powers such as section 1 of PACE (to find stolen or prohibited articles) and section 23 of the Misuse of Drugs Act 1971 (to find controlled drugs). This test must be applied to the particular circumstances in each case and is in two parts:

(i)   *Firstly*, the officer must have formed a *genuine* suspicion in their own mind that they will find the object for which the search power being exercised allows them to search (see Annex A, second column, for examples); and

(ii)   *Secondly*, the suspicion that the object will be found must be reasonable. This means that there must be an *objective* basis for that suspicion based on facts, information and/or intelligence which are relevant to the likelihood that the object in question will be found, so that a reasonable person would be entitled to reach the same conclusion based on the same facts and information and/or intelligence.

Officers must therefore be able to explain the basis for their suspicion by reference to intelligence or information about, or some specific behaviour by, the person concerned (see *paragraphs 3.8(d), 4.6* and *5.5*).

2.2A   The exercise of these stop and search powers depends on the likelihood that the person searched is in possession of an item for which they may be searched; it does not depend on the person concerned being suspected of committing an offence in relation to the object of the search. A police officer who has reasonable grounds to suspect that a person is in *innocent possession* of a stolen or prohibited article, controlled drug or other item for which the officer is empowered to search, may stop and search the person even though there would be no power of arrest. This would apply when a child under the age of criminal responsibility (10 years) is suspected of carrying any such item, even if they knew they had it. (See *Notes 1B* and *1BA*.)

Personal factors can never support reasonable grounds for suspicion

2.2B   Reasonable suspicion can never be supported on the basis of personal factors. This means that unless the police have information or intelligence which *provides a description* of a person suspected of carrying an article for which there is a power to stop and search, the following *cannot be used*, alone or in combination with each other, or in combination with any other factor, as the reason for stopping and searching any individual, including any vehicle which they are driving or are being carried in:

(a)   A person's physical appearance with regard, for example, to any of the 'relevant protected characteristics' set out in the Equality Act 2010, section 149, which are age, disability, gender reassignment, pregnancy and maternity, race, religion or belief, sex and sexual orientation (see *paragraph 1.1* and *Note 1A*), or the fact that the person is known to have a previous conviction; and

(b)   Generalisations or stereotypical images that certain groups or categories of people are more likely to be involved in criminal activity.

2.3   *Not used.*

Reasonable grounds for suspicion based on information and/or intelligence

2.4   Reasonable grounds for suspicion should normally be linked to accurate and current intelligence or information, relating to articles for which there is a power to stop and search, being carried by individuals or being in vehicles in any locality. This would include reports from members of the public or other officers describing:

- a person who has been seen carrying such an article or a vehicle in which such an article has been seen.

- crimes committed in relation to which such an article would constitute relevant evidence, for example, property stolen in a theft or burglary, an offensive weapon or bladed or sharply pointed article used to assault or threaten someone or an article used to cause criminal damage to property.

2.4A   Searches based on accurate and current intelligence or information are more likely to be effective. Targeting searches in a particular area at specified crime problems not only increases their effectiveness but also minimises inconvenience to law-abiding members of the public. It also helps in justifying the use of searches both to those who are searched and to the public. This does not, however, prevent stop and search powers being exercised in other locations where such powers may be exercised and reasonable suspicion exists.

2.5   *Not used.*

Reasonable grounds for suspicion and searching groups

2.6   Where there is reliable information or intelligence that members of a group or gang habitually carry knives unlawfully or weapons or controlled drugs, and wear a distinctive item of clothing or other means of identification in order to identify themselves as members of that group or gang, that distinctive item of clothing or other means of identification may provide reasonable grounds to stop and search any person believed to be a member of that group or gang. (See *Note 9.*)

2.6A   A similar approach would apply to particular organised protest groups where there is reliable information or intelligence:

(a)   that the group in question arranges meetings and marches to which one or more members bring articles intended to be used to cause criminal damage and/or injury to others in support of the group's aims;

(b)   that at one or more previous meetings or marches arranged by that group, such articles have been used and resulted in damage and/or injury; and

(c)   that on the subsequent occasion in question, one or more members of the group have brought with them such articles with similar intentions

These circumstances may provide reasonable grounds to stop and search any members of the group to find such articles (see *Note 9A*). See also *paragraphs 2.12 to 2.18, "Searches authorised under section 60 of the Criminal Justice and Public Order Act 1994"*, when serious violence is anticipated at meetings and marches.

Reasonable grounds for suspicion based on behaviour, time and location

2.6B   Reasonable suspicion may also exist without specific information or intelligence and on the basis of the behaviour of a person. For example, if an officer encounters someone on the street at night who is obviously trying to hide something, the officer may (depending on the other surrounding circumstances) base such suspicion on the fact that this kind of behaviour is often linked to stolen or prohibited articles being carried. An officer who forms the opinion that a person is acting suspiciously or that they appear to be nervous must be able to explain, with reference to specific aspects of the person's behaviour or conduct which they have observed, why they formed that opinion (see paragraphs 3.8(d) and 5.5). A hunch or instinct which cannot be explained or justified to an objective observer can never amount to reasonable grounds.

2.7   *Not used.*

2.8   *Not used.*

Securing public confidence and promoting community relations

2.8A   All police officers must recognise that searches are more likely to be effective, legitimate and secure public confidence when their reasonable grounds for suspicion are based on a range of objective factors. The overall use of these powers is more likely to be effective when up-to-date and accurate intelligence or information is communicated to officers and they are well-informed about local crime patterns. Local senior officers have a duty to ensure that those under their command who exercise stop and search powers have access to such information, and the officers exercising the powers have a duty to acquaint themselves with that information (see *paragraphs 5.1 to 5.6*).

Questioning to decide whether to carry out a search

2.9   An officer who has reasonable grounds for suspicion may detain the person concerned in order to carry out a search. Before carrying out the search the officer may ask questions about the person's behaviour or presence in circumstances which gave rise to the suspicion. As a result of questioning the detained person, the reasonable grounds for suspicion necessary to detain that person may be confirmed or, because of a satisfactory explanation, be dispelled. (See *Notes 2* and *3*.) Questioning may also reveal reasonable grounds to suspect the possession of a different kind of unlawful article from that originally suspected. Reasonable grounds for suspicion however cannot be provided retrospectively by such questioning during a person's detention or by refusal to answer any questions asked.

2.10   If, as a result of questioning before a search, or other circumstances which come to the attention of the officer, there cease to be reasonable grounds for suspecting that an article of a kind for which there is a power to stop and search is being carried, no search may take place. (See *Note 3*.) In the absence of any other lawful power to detain, the person is free to leave at will and must be so informed.

2.11   There is no power to stop or detain a person in order to find grounds for a search. Police officers have many encounters with members of the public which do not involve detaining people against their will and do not require any statutory power for an officer to speak to a person (see *paragraph 4.12* and *Note 1*). However, if reasonable grounds for suspicion emerge during such an encounter, the officer may detain the person to search them, even though no grounds existed when the encounter began. As soon as detention begins, and before searching, the officer must inform the person that they are being detained for the purpose of a search and take action in accordance with *paragraphs 3.8 to 3.11* under "*Steps to be taken prior to a search*".

(b) Searches authorised under section 60 of the Criminal Justice and Public Order Act 1994

2.12 Authority for a constable in uniform to stop and search under section 60 of the Criminal Justice and Public Order Act 1994 may be given if the authorising officer reasonably believes:

(a) that incidents involving serious violence may take place in any locality in the officer's police area, and it is expedient to use these powers to prevent their occurrence;

(b) that persons are carrying dangerous instruments or offensive weapons without good reason in any locality in the officer's police area; or

(c) that an incident involving serious violence has taken place in the officer's police area, a dangerous instrument or offensive weapon used in the incident is being carried by a person in any locality in that police area, and it is expedient to use these powers to find that instrument or weapon.

2.13 An authorisation under section 60 may only be given by an officer of the rank of inspector or above and in writing, or orally if paragraph 2.12(c) applies and it is not practicable to give the authorisation in writing. The authorisation (whether written or oral) must specify the grounds on which it was given, the locality in which the powers may be exercised and the period of time for which they are in force. The period authorised shall be no longer than appears reasonably necessary to prevent, or seek to prevent incidents of serious violence, or to deal with the problem of carrying dangerous instruments or offensive weapons or to find a dangerous instrument or offensive weapon that has been used. It may not exceed 24 hours. An oral authorisation given where paragraph 2.12(c) applies must be recorded in writing as soon as practicable. (See *Notes 10* to *13*.)

2.14 An inspector who gives an authorisation must, as soon as practicable, inform an officer of or above the rank of superintendent. This officer may direct that the authorisation shall be extended for a further 24 hours, if violence or the carrying of dangerous instruments or offensive weapons has occurred, or is suspected to have occurred, and the continued use of the powers is considered necessary to prevent or deal with further such activity or to find a dangerous instrument or offensive weapon used that has been used. That direction must be given in writing unless it is not practicable to do so, in which case it must be recorded in writing as soon as practicable afterwards. (See *Note 12*.)

2.14A The selection of persons and vehicles under section 60 to be stopped and, if appropriate, searched should reflect an objective assessment of the nature of the incident or weapon in question and the individuals and vehicles thought likely to be associated with that incident or those weapons (see *Notes 10* and *11*). The powers must not be used to stop and search persons and vehicles for reasons unconnected with the purpose of the authorisation. When selecting persons and vehicles to be stopped in response to a specific threat or incident, officers must take care not to discriminate unlawfully against anyone on the grounds of any of the protected characteristics set out in the Equality Act 2010. (See *paragraph 1.1*.)

2.14B   The driver of a vehicle which is stopped under section 60 and any person who is searched under section 60 are entitled to a written statement to that effect if they apply within twelve months from the day the vehicle was stopped or the person was searched. This statement is a record which states that the vehicle was stopped or (as the case may be) that the person was searched under section 60 and it may form part of the search record or be supplied as a separate record.

Powers to require removal of face coverings

2.15   Section 60AA of the Criminal Justice and Public Order Act 1994 also provides a power to demand the removal of disguises. The officer exercising the power must reasonably believe that someone is wearing an item wholly or mainly for the purpose of concealing identity. There is also a power to seize such items where the officer believes that a person intends to wear them for this purpose. There is no power to stop and search for disguises. An officer may seize any such item which is discovered when exercising a power of search for something else, or which is being carried, and which the officer reasonably believes is intended to be used for concealing anyone's identity. This power can only be used if an authorisation given under section 60 or under section 60AA, is in force. (See *Note 4*.)

2.16   Authority under section 60AA for a constable in uniform to require the removal of disguises and to seize them may be given if the authorising officer reasonably believes that activities may take place in any locality in the officer's police area that are likely to involve the commission of offences and it is expedient to use these powers to prevent or control these activities.

2.17   An authorisation under section 60AA may only be given by an officer of the rank of inspector or above, in writing, specifying the grounds on which it was given, the locality in which the powers may be exercised and the period of time for which they are in force. The period authorised shall be no longer than appears reasonably necessary to prevent, or seek to prevent the commission of offences. It may not exceed 24 hours. (See *Notes 10* to *13*.)

2.18   An inspector who gives an authorisation must, as soon as practicable, inform an officer of or above the rank of superintendent. This officer may direct that the authorisation shall be extended for a further 24 hours, if crimes have been committed, or are suspected to have been committed, and the continued use of the powers is considered necessary to prevent or deal with further such activity. This direction must also be given in writing at the time or as soon as practicable afterwards. (See *Note 12*.)

(c) *Not used*

(d) Searches under Schedule 5 to the Terrorism Prevention and Investigation Measures Act 2011

2.18A   Paragraph 3 of Schedule 5 to the TPIM Act 2011 allows a constable to detain an individual to be searched under the following powers:

(i)   paragraph 6(2)(a) when a TPIM notice is being, or has just been, served on the individual for the purpose of ascertaining whether there is anything on the individual that contravenes measures specified in the notice;

(ii)   paragraph 8(2)(a) in accordance with a warrant to search the individual issued by a justice of the peace in England and Wales, a sheriff in Scotland or a lay magistrate in Northern Ireland who is satisfied that a search is necessary for the purpose of determining whether an individual in respect of whom a TPIM notice is in force is complying with measures specified in the notice (see *paragraph 2.20*); and

(iii)   paragraph 10 to ascertain whether an individual in respect of whom a TPIM notice is in force is in possession of anything that could be used to threaten or harm any person.

See paragraph 2.1(e).

2.19   The exercise of the powers mentioned in *paragraph 2.18A* does not require the constable to have reasonable grounds to suspect that the individual:

(a)   has been, or is, contravening any of the measures specified in the TPIM notice; or

(b)   has on them anything which:

- in the case of the power in sub-paragraph (i), contravenes measures specified in the TPIM notice;

- in the case of the power in sub-paragraph (ii) is not complying with measures specified in the TPIM notice; or

- in the case of the power in sub-paragraph (iii), could be used to threaten or harm any person.

2.20   A search of an individual on warrant under the power mentioned in paragraph 2.18A(ii) must carried out within 28 days of the issue of the warrant and:

- the individual may be searched on one occasion only within that period;

- the search must take place at a reasonable hour unless it appears that this would frustrate the purposes of the search.

2.21   *Not used.*

2.22   *Not used.*

2.23   *Not used.*

2.24   *Not used.*

2.24A   *Not used.*

2.25   *Not used.*

2.26   The powers under Schedule 5 allow a constable to conduct a search of an individual only for specified purposes relating to a TPIM notice as set out above. However, anything found may be seized and retained if there are reasonable grounds for believing that it is or it contains evidence of any offence for use at a trial for that offence or to prevent it being concealed, lost, damaged, altered, or destroyed. However, this would not prevent a search being carried out under other search powers if, in the course of exercising these powers, the officer formed reasonable grounds for suspicion.

(e) Powers to search persons in the exercise of a power to search premises

2.27   The following powers to search premises also authorise the search of a person, not under arrest, who is found on the premises during the course of the search:

(a)   section 139B of the Criminal Justice Act 1988 under which a constable may enter school premises and search the premises and any person on those premises for any bladed or pointed article or offensive weapon;

(b)   under a warrant issued under section 23(3) of the Misuse of Drugs Act 1971 to search premises for drugs or documents but only if the warrant specifically authorises the search of persons found on the premises; and

(c)   under a search warrant or order issued under paragraph 1, 3 or 11 of Schedule 5 to the Terrorism Act 2000 to search premises and any person found there for material likely to be of substantial value to a terrorist investigation.

2.28   Before the power under section 139B of the Criminal Justice Act 1988 may be exercised, the constable must have reasonable grounds to suspect that an offence under section 139A or 139AA of the Criminal Justice Act 1988 (having a bladed or pointed article or offensive weapon on school premises) has been or is being committed. A warrant to search premises and persons found therein may be issued under section 23(3) of the Misuse of Drugs Act 1971 if there are reasonable grounds to suspect that controlled drugs or certain documents are in the possession of a person on the premises.

2.29   The powers in *paragraph 2.27* do not require prior specific grounds to suspect that the person to be searched is in possession of an item for which there is an existing power to search. However, it is still necessary to ensure that the selection and treatment of those searched under these powers is based upon objective factors connected with the search of the premises, and not upon personal prejudice.

3   Conduct of searches

3.1   All stops and searches must be carried out with courtesy, consideration and respect for the person concerned. This has a significant impact on public confidence in the police. Every reasonable effort must be made to minimise the embarrassment that a person being searched may experience. (See *Note 4*.)

3.2   The co-operation of the person to be searched must be sought in every case, even if the person initially objects to the search. A forcible search may be made only if it has been established that the person is unwilling to co-operate or resists. Reasonable force may be used as a last resort if necessary to conduct a search or to detain a person or vehicle for the purposes of a search.

3.3   The length of time for which a person or vehicle may be detained must be reasonable and kept to a minimum. Where the exercise of the power requires reasonable suspicion, the thoroughness and extent of a search must depend on what is suspected of being carried, and by whom. If the suspicion relates to a particular article which is seen to be slipped into a person's pocket, then, in the absence of other grounds for suspicion or an opportunity for the article to be moved elsewhere, the search must be confined to that pocket. In the case of a small article which can readily be concealed, such as a drug, and which might be concealed anywhere on the person, a more extensive search may be necessary. In the case of searches mentioned in *paragraph 2.1(b)* and *(d)*, which do not require reasonable grounds for suspicion, officers may make any reasonable search to look for items for which they are empowered to search. (See *Note 5.*)

3.4   The search must be carried out at or near the place where the person or vehicle was first detained. (See *Note 6.*)

3.5   There is no power to require a person to remove any clothing in public other than an outer coat, jacket or gloves, except under section 60AA of the Criminal Justice and Public Order Act 1994 (which empowers a constable to require a person to remove any item worn to conceal identity). (See *Notes 4* and *6.*) A search in public of a person's clothing which has not been removed must be restricted to superficial examination of outer garments. This does not, however, prevent an officer from placing his or her hand inside the pockets of the outer clothing, or feeling round the inside of collars, socks and shoes if this is reasonably necessary in the circumstances to look for the object of the search or to remove and examine any item reasonably suspected to be the object of the search. For the same reasons, subject to the restrictions on the removal of headgear, a person's hair may also be searched in public. (See *paragraphs 3.1* and *3.3.*)

3.6   Where on reasonable grounds it is considered necessary to conduct a more thorough search (e.g. by requiring a person to take off a T-shirt), this must be done out of public view, for example, in a police van unless *paragraph 3.7* applies, or police station if there is one nearby (see *Note 6.*) Any search involving the removal of more than an outer coat, jacket, gloves, headgear or footwear, or any other item concealing identity, may only be made by an officer of the same sex as the person searched and may not be made in the presence of anyone of the opposite sex unless the person being searched specifically requests it. (See *Code C Annex L* and *Notes 4* and *7.*)

3.7   Searches involving exposure of intimate parts of the body must not be conducted as a routine extension of a less thorough search, simply because nothing is found in the course of the initial search. Searches involving exposure of intimate parts of the body may be carried out only at a nearby police station or other nearby location which is out of public view (but not a police vehicle). These searches must be conducted in accordance with paragraph 11 of Annex A to Code C except that an intimate search mentioned in *paragraph 11(f) of Annex A* to Code C may not be authorised or carried out under any stop and search powers. The other provisions of Code C do not apply to the conduct and recording of searches of persons detained at police stations in the exercise of stop and search powers. (See *Note 7.*)

Steps to be taken prior to a search

3.8   Before any search of a detained person or attended vehicle takes place the officer must take reasonable steps, if not in uniform (see *paragraph 3.9*), to show their warrant card to the person to be searched or in charge of the vehicle to be searched and whether or not in uniform, to give that person the following information:

(a)   that they are being detained for the purposes of a search;

(b)   the officer's name (except in the case of enquiries linked to the investigation of terrorism, or otherwise where the officer reasonably believes that giving their name might put them in danger, in which case a warrant or other identification number shall be given) and the name of the police station to which the officer is attached;

(c)   the legal search power which is being exercised, and

(d)   a clear explanation of:

   (i)   the object of the search in terms of the article or articles for which there is a power to search; and

   (ii)   in the case of:

- the power under section 60 of the Criminal Justice and Public Order Act 1994 (see *paragraph 2.1(b)*), the nature of the power, the authorisation and the fact that it has been given;

- the powers under Schedule 5 to the Terrorism Prevention and Investigation Measures Act 2011 (see *paragraph 2.1(e)* and *2.18A*):
    ~ the fact that a TPIM notice is in force or, (in the case of paragraph 6(2)(a)) that a TPIM notice is being served;
    ~ the nature of the power being exercised.

    For a search under paragraph 8 of Schedule 5, the warrant must be produced and the person provided with a copy of it.

- all other powers requiring reasonable suspicion (see *paragraph 2.1(a)*), the grounds for that suspicion. This means explaining the basis for the suspicion by reference to information and/or intelligence about, or some specific behaviour by, the person concerned (see *paragraph 2.2*).

(e)   that they are entitled to a copy of the record of the search if one is made (see section 4 below) if they ask within 3 months from the date of the search and:

   (i)   if they are not arrested and taken to a police station as a result of the search and it is practicable to make the record on the spot, that immediately after the search is completed they will be given, if they request, either:

- a copy of the record; or

- a receipt which explains how they can obtain a copy of the full record or access to an electronic copy of the record; or

(ii) if they are arrested and taken to a police station as a result of the search, that the record will be made at the station as part of their custody record and they will be given, if they request, a copy of their custody record which includes a record of the search as soon as practicable whilst they are at the station. (See *Note 16.*)

3.9   Stops and searches under the power mentioned in *paragraph 2.1(b)* may be undertaken only by a constable in uniform.

3.10   The person should also be given information about police powers to stop and search and the individual's rights in these circumstances.

3.11   If the person to be searched, or in charge of a vehicle to be searched, does not appear to understand what is being said, or there is any doubt about the person's ability to understand English, the officer must take reasonable steps to bring information regarding the person's rights and any relevant provisions of this Code to his or her attention. If the person is deaf or cannot understand English and is accompanied by someone, then the officer must try to establish whether that person can interpret or otherwise help the officer to give the required information.

4   Recording requirements

(a) Searches which do not result in an arrest

4.1   When an officer carries out a search in the exercise of any power to which this Code applies and the search does not result in the person searched or person in charge of the vehicle searched being arrested and taken to a police station, a record must be made of it, electronically or on paper, unless there are exceptional circumstances which make this wholly impracticable (e.g. in situations involving public disorder or when the recording officer's presence is urgently required elsewhere). If a record is to be made, the officer carrying out the search must make the record on the spot unless this is not practicable, in which case, the officer must make the record as soon as practicable after the search is completed. (See *Note 16.*)

4.2   If the record is made at the time, the person who has been searched or who is in charge of the vehicle that has been searched must be asked if they want a copy and if they do, they must be given immediately, either:

- a copy of the record; or
- a receipt which explains how they can obtain a copy of the full record or access to an electronic copy of the record.

4.2A   An officer is not required to provide a copy of the full record or a receipt at the time if they are called to an incident of higher priority. (See *Note 21.*)

(b) Searches which result in an arrest

4.2B   If a search in the exercise of any power to which this Code applies results in a person being arrested and taken to a police station, the officer carrying out the search is responsible for ensuring that a record of the search is made as part of their custody record. The custody officer must then ensure that the person is asked if they want a copy of the record and, if they do, that they are given a copy as soon as practicable. (See *Note 16.*)

(c) Record of search

4.3   The record of a search must always include the following information:

(a) A note of the self defined ethnicity, and if different, the ethnicity as perceived by the officer making the search, of the person searched or of the person in charge of the vehicle searched (as the case may be) (see *Note 18*);

(b) The date, time and place the person or vehicle was searched (see *Note 6*);

(c) The object of the search in terms of the article or articles for which there is a power to search;

(d) In the case of:

- the power under section 60 of the Criminal Justice and Public Order Act 1994 (see *paragraph 2.1(b)*), the nature of the power, the authorisation and the fact that it has been given (see *Note 17*);

- the powers under Schedule 5 to the Terrorism Prevention and Investigation Measures Act 2011 (see *paragraphs 2.1(e)* and *2.18A*):

  ~ the fact that a TPIM notice is in force or, (in the case of paragraph 6(2)(a)), that a TPIM notice is being served;

  ~ the nature of the power, and

  ~ for a search under paragraph 8, the date the search warrant was issued, the fact that the warrant was produced and a copy of it provided and the warrant must also be endorsed by the constable executing it to state whether anything was found and whether anything was seized, and

- all other powers requiring reasonable suspicion (see *paragraph 2.1(a)*), the grounds for that suspicion.

(e) subject to paragraph 3.8(b), the identity of the officer carrying out the search. (See *Note 15*.)

4.3A   For the purposes of completing the search record, there is no requirement to record the name, address and date of birth of the person searched or the person in charge of a vehicle which is searched. The person is under no obligation to provide this information and they should not be asked to provide it for the purpose of completing the record.

4.4   Nothing in *paragraph 4.3* requires the names of police officers to be shown on the search record or any other record required to be made under this Code in the case of enquiries linked to the investigation of terrorism or otherwise where an officer reasonably believes that recording names might endanger the officers. In such cases the record must show the officers' warrant or other identification number and duty station.

4.5   A record is required for each person and each vehicle searched. However, if a person is in a vehicle and both are searched, and the object and grounds of the search are the same, only one record need be completed. If more than one person in a vehicle is searched, separate records for each search of a person must be made. If only a vehicle is searched, the self-defined ethnic background of the person in charge of the vehicle must be recorded, unless the vehicle is unattended.

4.6   The record of the grounds for making a search must, briefly but informatively, explain the reason for suspecting the person concerned, by reference to information and/or intelligence about, or some specific behaviour by, the person concerned (see *paragraph 2.2*).

4.7   Where officers detain an individual with a view to performing a search, but the need to search is eliminated as a result of questioning the person detained, a search should not be carried out and a record is not required. (See *paragraph 2.10* and *Notes 3* and *22A*.)

4.8   After searching an unattended vehicle, or anything in or on it, an officer must leave a notice in it (or on it, if things on it have been searched without opening it) recording the fact that it has been searched.

4.9   The notice must include the name of the police station to which the officer concerned is attached and state where a copy of the record of the search may be obtained and how (if applicable) an electronic copy may be accessed and where any application for compensation should be directed.

4.10   The vehicle must if practicable be left secure.

4.10A   *Not used.*

4.10B   *Not used.*

Recording of encounters not governed by statutory powers

4.11   *Not used*

4.12   There is no national requirement for an officer who requests a person in a public place to account for themselves, i.e. their actions, behaviour, presence in an area or possession of anything, to make any record of the encounter or to give the person a receipt. (See *paragraph 2.11* and *Notes 22A* and *22B*.)

4.12A   *Not used.*

4.13   *Not used.*

4.14   *Not used.*

4.15   *Not used.*

4.16   *Not used.*

4.17   *Not used.*

4.18   *Not used.*

4.19   *Not used.*

4.20   *Not used.*

5 Monitoring and supervising the use of stop and search powers

General

5.1 Any misuse of stop and search powers is likely to be harmful to policing and lead to mistrust of the police by the local community and by the public in general. Supervising officers must monitor the use of stop and search powers and should consider in particular whether there is any evidence that they are being exercised on the basis of stereotyped images or inappropriate generalisations. Supervising officers must satisfy themselves that the practice of officers under their supervision in stopping, searching and recording is fully in accordance with this Code. Supervisors must also examine whether the records reveal any trends or patterns which give cause for concern and, if so, take appropriate action to address this. (See *paragraph 2.8A*.)

5.2 Senior officers with area or force-wide responsibilities must also monitor the broader use of stop and search powers and, where necessary, take action at the relevant level.

5.3 Supervision and monitoring must be supported by the compilation of comprehensive statistical records of stops and searches at force, area and local level. Any apparently disproportionate use of the powers by particular officers or groups of officers or in relation to specific sections of the community should be identified and investigated.

5.4 In order to promote public confidence in the use of the powers, forces, in consultation with police and crime commissioners, must make arrangements for the records to be scrutinised by representatives of the community, and to explain the use of the powers at a local level. (See *Note 19*.)

Suspected misuse of powers by individual officers

5.5 Police supervisors must monitor the use of stop and search powers by individual officers to ensure that they are being applied appropriately and lawfully. Monitoring takes many forms, such as direct supervision of the exercise of the powers, examining stop and search records (particularly examining the officer's documented reasonable grounds for suspicion) and asking the officer to account for the way in which they conducted and recorded particular searches or through complaints about a stop and search that an officer has carried out.

5.6 Where a supervisor identifies issues with the way that an officer has used a stop and search power, the facts of the case will determine whether the standards of professional behaviour as set out in the Code of Ethics (see http://www.college.police. uk/en/20972.htm) have been breached and which formal action is pursued. Improper use might be a result of poor performance or a conduct matter, which will require the supervisor to take appropriate action such as performance or misconduct procedures. It is imperative that supervisors take both timely and appropriate action to deal with all such cases that come to their notice.

Notes for guidance

Officers exercising stop and search powers

1 *This Code does not affect the ability of an officer to speak to or question a person in the ordinary course of the officer's duties without detaining the person or exercising any element of compulsion. It is not the purpose of the code to prohibit such encounters*

between the police and the community with the co-operation of the person concerned and neither does it affect the principle that all citizens have a duty to help police officers to prevent crime and discover offenders. This is a civic rather than a legal duty; but when a police officer is trying to discover whether, or by whom, an offence has been committed he or she may question any person from whom useful information might be obtained, subject to the restrictions imposed by Code C. A person's unwillingness to reply does not alter this entitlement, but in the absence of a power to arrest, or to detain in order to search, the person is free to leave at will and cannot be compelled to remain with the officer.

1A   *In paragraphs 1.1 and 2.2B(a), the 'relevant protected characteristics' are: age, disability, gender reassignment, pregnancy and maternity, race, religion or belief, sex and sexual orientation.*

1B   *Innocent possession means that the person does [not] have the guilty knowledge that they are carrying an unlawful item which is required before an arrest on suspicion that the person has committed an offence in respect of the item sought (if arrest is necessary - see PACE Code G) and/or a criminal prosecution) can be considered. It is not uncommon for children under the age of criminal responsibility to be used by older children and adults to carry stolen property, drugs and weapons and, in some cases, firearms, for the criminal benefit of others, either:*

- *in the hope that police may not suspect they are being used for carrying the items; or*

- *knowing that if they are suspected of being couriers and are stopped and searched, they cannot be arrested or prosecuted for any criminal offence.*

Stop and search powers therefore allow the police to intervene effectively to break up criminal gangs and groups that use young children to further their criminal activities.

1BA   *Whenever a child under 10 is suspected of carrying unlawful items for someone else, or is found in circumstances which suggest that their welfare and safety may be at risk, the facts should be reported and actioned in accordance with established force safeguarding procedures. This will be in addition to treating them as a potentially vulnerable or intimidated witness in respect of their status as a witness to the serious criminal offence(s) committed by those using them as couriers. Safeguarding considerations will also apply to other persons aged under 18 who are stopped and searched under any of the powers to which this Code applies. See paragraph 1.1 with regard to the requirement under the Children Act 2004, section 11, for chief police officers and other specified persons and bodies, to ensure that in the discharge of their functions, they have regard to the need to safeguard and promote the welfare of all persons under the age of 18.*

2   *In some circumstances preparatory questioning may be unnecessary, but in general a brief conversation or exchange will be desirable not only as a means of avoiding unsuccessful searches, but to explain the grounds for the stop/search, to gain co-operation and reduce any tension there might be surrounding the stop/search.*

3   *Where a person is lawfully detained for the purpose of a search, but no search in the event takes place, the detention will not thereby have been rendered unlawful.*

4   *Many people customarily cover their heads or faces for religious reasons - for example, Muslim women, Sikh men, Sikh or Hindu women, or Rastafarian men or women. A police officer cannot order the removal of a head or face covering except where there is reason to believe that the item is being worn by the individual wholly or mainly for the purpose of disguising identity, not simply because it disguises identity. Where there may be religious sensitivities about ordering the removal of such an item, the officer should permit the item to be removed out of public view. Where practicable, the item should be removed in the presence of an officer of the same sex as the person and out of sight of anyone of the opposite sex (see Code C Annex L).*

5   *A search of a person in public should be completed as soon as possible.*

6   *A person may be detained under a stop and search power at a place other than where the person was first detained, only if that place, be it a police station or elsewhere, is nearby. Such a place should be located within a reasonable travelling distance using whatever mode of travel (on foot or by car) is appropriate. This applies to all searches under stop and search powers, whether or not they involve the removal of clothing or exposure of intimate parts of the body (see paragraphs 3.6 and 3.7) or take place in or out of public view. It means, for example, that a search under the stop and search power in section 23 of the Misuse of Drugs Act 1971 which involves the compulsory removal of more than a person's outer coat, jacket or gloves cannot be carried out unless a place which is both nearby the place they were first detained and out of public view, is available. If a search involves exposure of intimate parts of the body and a police station is not nearby, particular care must be taken to ensure that the location is suitable in that it enables the search to be conducted in accordance with the requirements of paragraph 11 of Annex A to Code C.*

7   *A search in the street itself should be regarded as being in public for the purposes of paragraphs 3.6 and 3.7 above, even though it may be empty at the time a search begins. Although there is no power to require a person to do so, there is nothing to prevent an officer from asking a person voluntarily to remove more than an outer coat, jacket or gloves in public.*

8   *Not used.*

9   *Other means of identification might include jewellery, insignias, tattoos or other features which are known to identify members of the particular gang or group.*

9A   *A decision to search individuals believed to be members of a particular group or gang must be judged on a case by case basis according to the circumstances applicable at the time of the proposed searches and in particular, having regard to:*

    (a)   the number of items suspected of being carried;

    (b)   the nature of those items and the risk they pose; and

    (c)   the number of individuals to be searched.

A group search will only be justified if it is a necessary and proportionate approach based on the facts and having regard to the nature of the suspicion in these cases. The extent and thoroughness of the searches must not be excessive.

The size of the group and the number of individuals it is proposed to search will be a key factor and steps should be taken to identify those who are to be searched to avoid unnecessary inconvenience to unconnected members of the public who are also present.

The onus is on the police to be satisfied and to demonstrate that their approach to the decision to search is in pursuit of a legitimate aim, necessary and proportionate.

Authorising officers

10   *The powers under section 60 are separate from and additional to the normal stop and search powers which require reasonable grounds to suspect an individual of carrying an offensive weapon (or other article). Their overall purpose is to prevent serious violence and the widespread carrying of weapons which might lead to persons being seriously injured by disarming potential offenders or finding weapons that have been used in circumstances where other powers would not be sufficient. They should not therefore be used to replace or circumvent the normal powers for dealing with routine crime problems. A particular example might be an authorisation to prevent serious violence or the carrying of offensive weapons at a sports event by rival team supporters when the expected general appearance and age range of those likely to be responsible, alone, would not be sufficiently distinctive to support reasonable suspicion (see paragraph 2.6). The purpose of the powers under section 60AA is to prevent those involved in intimidatory or violent protests using face coverings to disguise identity.*

11   *Authorisations under section 60 require a reasonable belief on the part of the authorising officer. This must have an objective basis, for example: intelligence or relevant information such as a history of antagonism and violence between particular groups; previous incidents of violence at, or connected with, particular events or locations; a significant increase in knife-point robberies in a limited area; reports that individuals are regularly carrying weapons in a particular locality; information following an incident in which weapons were used about where the weapons might be found or in the case of section 60AA previous incidents of crimes being committed while wearing face coverings to conceal identity.*

12   *It is for the authorising officer to determine the period of time during which the powers mentioned in paragraph 2.1(b) may be exercised. The officer should set the minimum period he or she considers necessary to deal with the risk of violence, the carrying of knives or offensive weapons, or to find dangerous instruments or weapons that have been used. A direction to extend the period authorised under the powers mentioned in paragraph 2.1(b) may be given only once. Thereafter further use of the powers requires a new authorisation.*

13   *It is for the authorising officer to determine the geographical area in which the use of the powers is to be authorised. In doing so the officer may wish to take into account factors such as the nature and venue of the anticipated incident or the incident which has taken place, the number of people who may be in the immediate area of that incident, their access to surrounding areas and the anticipated or actual level of violence. The officer should not set a geographical area which is wider than that he or she believes necessary for the purpose of preventing anticipated violence, the carrying of knives*

or offensive weapons, or for finding a dangerous instrument or weapon that has been used or, in the case of section 60AA, the prevention of commission of offences. It is particularly important to ensure that constables exercising such powers are fully aware of the locality within which they may be used. The officer giving the authorisation should therefore specify either the streets which form the boundary of the locality or a divisional boundary if appropriate, within the force area. If the power is to be used in response to a threat or incident that straddles police force areas, an officer from each of the forces concerned will need to give an authorisation.

14   *Not used.*

Recording

15   *Where a stop and search is conducted by more than one officer the identity of all the officers engaged in the search must be recorded on the record. Nothing prevents an officer who is present but not directly involved in searching from completing the record during the course of the encounter.*

16   *When the search results in the person searched or in charge of a vehicle which is searched being arrested, the requirement to make the record of the search as part of the person's custody record does not apply if the person is granted "street bail" after arrest (see section 30A of PACE) to attend a police station and is not taken in custody to the police station An arrested person's entitlement to a copy of the search record which is made as part of their custody record does not affect their entitlement to a copy of their custody record or any other provisions of PACE Code C section 2 (Custody records).*

17   *It is important for monitoring purposes to specify when authority is given for exercising the stop and search power under section 60 of the Criminal Justice and Public Order Act 1994.*

18   *Officers should record the self-defined ethnicity of every person stopped according to the categories used in the 2001 census question listed in Annex B. The person should be asked to select one of the five main categories representing broad ethnic groups and then a more specific cultural background from within this group. The ethnic classification should be coded for recording purposes using the coding system in Annex B. An additional "Not stated" box is available but should not be offered to respondents explicitly. Officers should be aware and explain to members of the public, especially where concerns are raised, that this information is required to obtain a true picture of stop and search activity and to help improve ethnic monitoring, tackle discriminatory practice, and promote effective use of the powers. If the person gives what appears to the officer to be an "incorrect" answer (e.g. a person who appears to be white states that they are black), the officer should record the response that has been given and then record their own perception of the person's ethnic background by using the PNC classification system. If the "Not stated" category is used the reason for this must be recorded on the form.*

19   *Arrangements for public scrutiny of records should take account of the right to confidentiality of those stopped and searched. Anonymised forms and/or statistics generated from records should be the focus of the examinations by members of the*

public. The groups that are consulted should always include children and young persons.

20   *Not used.*

21   *In situations where it is not practicable to provide a written copy of the record or immediate access to an electronic copy of the record or a receipt of the search at the time (see paragraph 4.2A above), the officer should consider giving the person details of the station which they may attend for a copy of the record. A receipt may take the form of a simple business card which includes sufficient information to locate the record should the person ask for copy, for example, the date and place of the search, and a reference number or the name of the officer who carried out the search (unless paragraph 4.4 applies).*

22   *Not used.*

22A   *Where there are concerns which make it necessary to monitor any local disproportionality, forces have discretion to direct officers to record the self-defined ethnicity of persons they request to account for themselves in a public place or who they detain with a view to searching but do not search. Guidance should be provided locally and efforts made to minimise the bureaucracy involved. Records should be closely monitored and supervised in line with paragraphs 5.1 to 5.6, and forces can suspend or re-instate recording of these encounters as appropriate.*

22B   *A person who is asked to account for themselves should, if they request, be given information about how they can report their dissatisfaction about how they have been treated.*

Definition of offensive weapon

23   *'Offensive weapon' is defined as "any article made or adapted for use for causing injury to the person, or intended by the person having it with him for such use by him or by someone else". There are three categories of offensive weapons: those made for causing injury to the person; those adapted for such a purpose; and those not so made or adapted, but carried with the intention of causing injury to the person. A firearm, as defined by section 57 of the Firearms Act 1968, would fall within the definition of offensive weapon if any of the criteria above apply.*

24   *Not used.*

25   *Not used.*

ANNEX A SUMMARY OF MAIN STOP AND SEARCH POWERS TO WHICH CODE A APPLIES

THIS TABLE RELATES TO STOP AND SEARCH POWERS ONLY. INDIVIDUAL STATUTES BELOW MAY CONTAIN OTHER POLICE POWERS OF ENTRY, SEARCH AND SEIZURE

POWER	OBJECT OF SEARCH	EXTENT OF SEARCH	WHERE EXERCISABLE
Unlawful articles general			
1. Public Stores Act 1875, s6.	HM Stores stolen or unlawfully obtained.	Persons, vehicles and vessels.	Anywhere where the constabulary powers are exercisable.
2. Firearms Act 1968, s47	Firearms	Persons and vehicles	A public place, or anywhere in the case of reasonable suspicion of offences of carrying firearms with criminal intent or trespassing with firearms.
3. Misuse of Drugs Act 1971, s23	Controlled drugs	Persons and vehicles.	Anywhere.
4. Customs and Excise Management Act 1979, s163	Goods: (a) on which duty has not been paid; (b) being unlawfully removed, imported or exported; (c) otherwise liable to forfeiture to HM Revenue and Customs.	Vehicles and vessels only.	Anywhere.
5. Aviation Security Act 1982, s24B. *Note: This power applies throughout the UK but the provisions of this Code will apply only when the power is exercised at an aerodrome situated in England and Wales.*	Stolen articles or articles made, adapted or intended for use in the course of/in connection with conduct which constitutes an offence in the part of the UK where the aerodrome is situated or would so do, if it occurred there.	Persons, vehicles, aircraft. Anything in or on a vehicle or aircraft.	Any part of an aerodrome.

POWER	OBJECT OF SEARCH	EXTENT OF SEARCH	WHERE EXERCISABLE
6. Police and Criminal Evidence Act 1984, s1.	Stolen goods;	Persons and vehicles.	Where there is public access.
	Articles made, adapted or intended for use in the course of or in connection with, certain offences under the Theft Act 1968, Fraud Act and Criminal Damage Act 1971;	Persons and vehicles.	Where there is public access.
	Offensive weapons, Bladed or sharply-pointed articles (except folding pocket knives with a blade cutting edge not exceeding 3 inches);	Persons and vehicles.	Where there is public access.
	Fireworks: Category 4 (display grade) fireworks if possession prohibited, Adult fireworks in possession of a person under 18 in a public place.	Persons and vehicles.	Where there is public access.
7. Sporting events (Control of Alcohol etc.) Act 1985, s7.	Intoxicating liquor.	Persons, coaches and trains.	Designated sports grounds or coaches and trains travelling to or from a designated sporting event.
8. Crossbows Act 1987, s4.	Crossbows or parts of crossbows (except crossbows with a draw weight of less than 1.4 kilograms).	Persons and vehicles.	Anywhere except dwellings.
9. Criminal Justice Act 1988 s139B.	Offensive weapons, bladed or sharply pointed article.	Persons.	School premises.
**Evidence of game and wildlife offences**			
10. Poaching Prevention Act 1862, s2.	Game or poaching equipment.	Persons and vehicles.	A public place.
11. Deer Act 1991, s12.	Evidence of offences under the Act.	Persons and vehicles.	Anywhere except dwellings.
12. Conservation of Seals Act 1970, s4.	Seals or hunting equipment	Vehicles only	Anywhere.

POWER	OBJECT OF SEARCH	EXTENT OF SEARCH	WHERE EXERCISABLE
13. Protection of Badgers Act 1992, s11.	Evidence of offences under the Act.	Persons and vehicles.	Anywhere.
14. Wildlife and Countryside Act 1981, s19.	Evidence of wildlife offences.	Persons and vehicles.	Anywhere except dwellings.
Other			
15. Paragraphs 6 & 8 of Schedule 5 to the Terrorism Prevention and Investigation Measures Act 2011.	Anything that contravenes measures specified in a TPIM notice.	Persons in respect of whom a TPIM notice is being served or is in force.	Anywhere.
16. Paragraph 10 of Schedule 5 to the Terrorism Prevention and Investigation Measures Act 2011.	Anything that could be used to threaten or harm any person.	Persons in respect of whom a TPIM notice is in force.	Anywhere.
17. *Not used*			
18. *Not used*			
19. Section 60 Criminal Justice and Public Order Act 1994.	Offensive weapons or dangerous instruments to prevent incidents of serious violence or to deal with the carrying of such items or find such items which have been used in incidents of serious violence.	Persons and vehicles.	Anywhere within a locality authorised under subsection (1).

ANNEX B SELF-DEFINED ETHNIC CLASSIFICATION CATEGORIES

White		***W***
A.	*White – British*	*W1*
B.	*White – Irish*	*W2*
C.	*Any other White background*	*W9*
Mixed		***M***
D.	*White and Black Caribbean*	*M1*
E.	*White and Black African*	*M2*
F.	*White and Asian*	*M3*
G.	*Any other Mixed Background*	*M9*
Asian/Asian – British		***A***
H.	*Asian – Indian*	*A1*
I.	*Asian – Pakistani*	*A2*
J.	*Asian – Bangladeshi*	*A3*
K.	*Any other Asian background*	*A9*
Black/Black – British		***B***
L.	*Black – Caribbean*	*B1*
M.	*Black African*	*B2*
N.	*Any other Black background*	*B9*
Other		***O***
O.	*Chinese*	*01*
P.	*Any other*	*09*
Not Stated		**NS**

ANNEX C SUMMARY OF POWERS OF COMMUNITY SUPPORT OFFICERS TO SEARCH AND SEIZE

The following is a summary of the search and seizure powers that may be exercised by a community support officer (CSO) who has been designated with the relevant powers in accordance with Part 4 of the Police Reform Act 2002.

When exercising any of these powers, a CSO must have regard to any relevant provisions of this Code, including section 3 governing the conduct of searches and the steps to be taken prior to a search.

1.   ***Not used***

2.   **Powers to search requiring the consent of the person and seizure**

A CSO may detain a person using reasonable force where necessary as set out in Part 1 of Schedule 4 to the Police Reform Act 2002. If the person has been lawfully detained, the CSO may search the person provided that person gives consent to such a search in relation to the following:

Designation	Powers conferred	Object of Search	Extent of Search	Where Exercisable
1. Police Reform Act 2002, Schedule 4, paragraphs 7 and 7A.	(a) Criminal Justice and Police Act 2001, s12(2).	(a) Alcohol or a container for alcohol.	(a) Persons.	(a) Designated public place.
	(b) Confiscation of Alcohol (Young Persons) Act 1997, s1	(b) Alcohol.	(b) Persons under 18 years old.	(b) Public place.
	(c) Children and Young Persons Act 1933, s7(3).	(c) Tobacco or cigarette papers.	(c) Persons under 16 years old found smoking.	(c) Public place.

3. Powers to search not requiring the consent of the person and seizure

A CSO may detain a person using reasonable force where necessary as set out in Part 1 of Schedule 4 to the Police Reform Act 2002. If the person has been lawfully detained, the CSO may search the person without the need for that person's consent in relation to the following:

Designation	Power conferred	Object of Search	Extent of Search	Where Exercisable
Police Reform Act 2002, Schedule 4 paragraph 2A.,	Police and Criminal Evidence Act 1984, s.32.	(a) Objects that might be used to cause physical injury to the person or the CSO. (b) Items that might be used to assist escape.	Persons made subject to a requirement to wait.	Any place where the requirement to wait has been made.

4. Powers to seize without consent

This power applies when drugs are found in the course of any search mentioned above.

Designation	Power conferred	Object of Seizure	Where Exercisable
Police Reform Act 2002, Schedule 4, paragraph 7B.	Police Reform Act 2002, Schedule 4, paragraph 7B.	Controlled drugs in a person's possession.	Any place where the person is in possession of the drug.

ANNEX D – Deleted.

ANNEX E – Deleted.

ANNEX F   ESTABLISHING GENDER OF PERSONS FOR THE PURPOSE OF SEARCHING

See *Code C Annex L*